From the Moon, To the Sun and back again

Angelica Gomez

Presentation by *BookLeaf Publishing*

Web: www.bookleafpub.com

E-mail: info@bookleafpub.com

ISBN: 9789357745154

First edition 2023

Fool's Journey

The beginnings of the Fool
Conscious awareness of the Magician
Unconscious awareness of the High Priestess
Nurtured by the Empress
Protected by the Emperor
Conformity with the Hierophant
Finding value in the Lovers
Self-assertion with the Chariot
Compassion in Strength
Inner guidance with the Hermit
A turning point on the Wheel of Fortune
Responsibility of truth with Justice
New perspective of the Hanged Man
Transition with Death
Combination of Temperance
Restriction of the Devil
Downfall to the Tower
Purpose to the Star
Subconscious with the Moon
Vitality from the Sun
Rebirth from Judgement
Intergrate with the World

Fool's Lesson

O, I am the Fortune's Fool
Manipulated by the Magician
Disconnected with the High Priestess
Dependant on the Empress
Dominated by the Emperor
Challenging the Hierophant
Creating disharmony with the Lovers
Lacking discipline with the Chariot
Doubting inner Strength
Finding isolation with the Hermit
Breaking cycles with the Wheel of Fortune
Unfair with Justice
Stalling the Hanged Man
Transformation of Death
Excess Temperance
Exploring the Devil
Fearing the Tower
Disconnected from the Star
Confused with the Moon
Optimistic of the Sun
Ignoring the call of Judgement
Personal clousure of the World

Ocean's Song

I met a siren in real life
  Appealing and alluring on the surface
 Ultimately deceptive, dangerous, and
destructive
 Once the job was done you left without a fight
 Came in like a black hole and consumed my
light
 Can't believe I loved you with all my might
 Not even mad just disappointed
 Why would you lie?
 Have the audacity to ask me to look into your
eyes
 Put my hand on your heart and hope to die
 Thats what you said right?
 I can't live without you, won't be without you
 Your everything I need to breathe
 Damn do you feed that script to everyone you
meet?
 I was entrapped by your siren song
 Until I made a jump that made me deaf
 With all your ego you sang louder until your
throat blew
 I can finally see right through you

Sheep's Clothing

Came to me like a wolf in the night
Hungry, cold, no pack in tow
Eyes that appear flat, dead, cold
On a hunt to feed the ego
Unrelenting, unprincipled, inculpable
Testing their prey like an opportunist
Sensing weakness and vulnerability
Thriving on the element of surprise
Cautiously they stalk and wait to strike
Making sure they don't miss
Pouncing on you like a bad kiss
Full of remiss
A sense of disillusionment
Be careful when they strike
If they fail they will trail you
Making sure to completely derail you
Tire you out til you admit defeat
Then devour you like a feast

Remiss

Met a real life devil
 A succubus of sorts
 Came in with a nice smile and big eyes
 Smooth words and charming energy
 Never thought they would be my rise and my
demise
 Came in like a nuclear love bomb and declared
war
 Left my soul feeling like "WHAT THE
FUCK!?"
 Left my mind like spongbob "WHATS MY
NAME!?"
 Left my heart feeling like "YOU DID IT
AGAIN!?"
 Have my lips wondering "Who are you?"
 Have my spirit wondering "Who did we let in?"
 They replaced the face of my traumas
 They made me question energy all because their
words matched but action did not
 They made me realize peace comes from self
not in the disguise of a wolf in sheeps clothing
 They attacked me spiritually but all they did
was remind me of how powerful I really am

Always Knew

How could I have been such a fool to had
opened up my soul so easily?
 Why did I fall so deeply for a energy that wasn't
meant for me?
 Ive always trusted my cards but seems they lied
to me
 Maybe my own mind created something I
wanted it to be.
 I so desperately wanted to believe in you
 Thats not true
 Part of me always knew
 But I let my heart fall apart
 Let my mind feel numb on overload
 My spirit was lost
 Learning you- Lesson
 Losing you- Blessing

Inside Me

She's always been afraid
 Full of fear and insecurities
 Dying inside
 Flying outside
 She's worn the mask for so long, how can
anyone see more than who she portrays to be?
 Stitched together by trauma
 Bonded by what broke her
 Weighted by the chains she can't release from
 She wants to be as free as a bird
 As light as a feather
 To have her head in the clouds
 Feet planted deeply into the ground
 Imaginative and grounded
 Yet full of illusions and floating
 Covered in scars she hopes no one can see
 They are more than skin deep
 Bleeding from the inside out
 Drowning from the grief shes experienced
 She's begging Save me
 She's tired and worn down
 Broken hearted and numb to words
 A butterfly appears from the spirits
 Creating a butterfly effect
 Exposing light from darkness

Turning chaos to calmness
Just like a quiet thunderstorm
Turns into a double rainbow

See Me

Look at me
Really look at me
Don't look past me
Don't look through me
See my beauty even when I don't feel it
See my intelligence even when I don't show it
Feel my energy
Watch my aura bloom
Take a extra look
Or two
I exist
I am here
A vessel of completion
A vision of compilations
Defined as unusual
Redefined as unexceptionable

Overload

Pour my Cup
 Throw one in the air
 Pen to Paper
 Heart to Thought
 "What was I Thinking?"
 Woulda, Coulda, Shoulda
 Did I?
 Have I?
 Can I?
 Phone's Ringing
 This house is too loud
 I can't think
 TV's playing my favorite movie
 It's playing that one scene
 Where was I?
 Woulda, Coulda, Shoulda
 Heart to Thought
 Pen to Paper
 Throw one in the air
 Pour my cup

Heart Eyes

Blessed with abundance
Find solace in what the universe brings
Energy graciously flows through you
Everything in life is beauty
Chaos creates art
Darkness creates a background
Your light is its best feature
Create a masterpiece
Find that even when you can't see you
You are Beautiful
Find that even when you can't feel you
You are Glowing
Gracious
Meticulous
Perfectly Imperfect
A work of Art

Temperance

I learned my power from the Universe
It has guided me towards dark and light
Blessed me and disgraced me
Given me happiness and heartbreak
Taught me gratitude and ungratefulness
It has reminded me of time
The value of minutes in a day
Days in a month
Months in a year
It has been modest and blunt
Has turned my scars to works of art
Has turned my tears to watercolor
Cut me deep yet never saw me bleed
The universe has always been what I need

Free Falling

What are we doing here?
Should we see where this goes?
Down the rabbit hole we go
Where we fall, nobody knows
Can I trust you with my all?
Drink me
Eat me
Did your heart grow tall?
Did your mind shrink?
Was the combination too much to take in?
Lets peek through the peephole
Not quite sure we're the right size yet
The white rabbit appears
"Your late, your late, your late"

Fear

Disconnected with my subconscious awareness
Misaligned with my intuition
I believe more in the voices of my mind
Than with my heart
The thought of illustrations created by illusions
Ideas created by the power of magical forces
Manifesting irrational self-limiting beliefs
The belief that emotions are weak
Generational curses creeping in
Gotta turn that pain to power
Power comes from within
From your own voice inside your mind
From your own truths
Do not let chaos reside

Magic

There's power in words
Magic in the tone
Even silence speaks volumes
There's many reasons
To tell our story
To help others understand us
By cause or explanation
Our thoughts and our words
To find reason
Searching for truth
Reason comes from the power of the mind
Reason is not logic but the start of it
Not every reason we find makes sense

Writer's Block

A fog
A quiet storm
Million thoughts racing
Putting pen to paper
Nothing
Road block
Detour
Infinity loop of unprocessed thoughts
A sentence with no meaning
How many times did I write this?
Erase
Tear page
Try again
Nothing
A fight between idea and reality

Versus

Rage is when you react
 When you've held it in for too long and you
need to let it out
 Impulsive
 Explosive
 Impatient
 Anger is when you feel it
 Sometimes never boiling to the surface
 Surpresive
 Hidden
 One requires a thought
 Other requires effort
 They differentiate in action

Half Empty Half Full

Million words
 Million thoughts
 Are they from this world or extraterrestrial?
 Feeling stuck in a Inbetween of what's meant
for me
 Wondering where I fall
 When my body is weak and my mind
incomplete
 How can I win?
 The beauty of the fine line between strong and
weak
 The constant change
 The moments we miss
 The ones we never try to forget
 Even the moon and the sun change their point
of view
 Even time likes to play the fool
 A million vibes
 A million lessons

To the moon, from the sun and back again

To the moon
 Thank you
 For being that face in the moon
 For listening to me forgive those who wronged
me
 For giving me new energy when you are new
and helping me cleanse when you are full
 From the Sun
 Thank you for providing me with warmth
 Being my light on my dark days
 I'll always be here
 And back again